P9-DGK-111

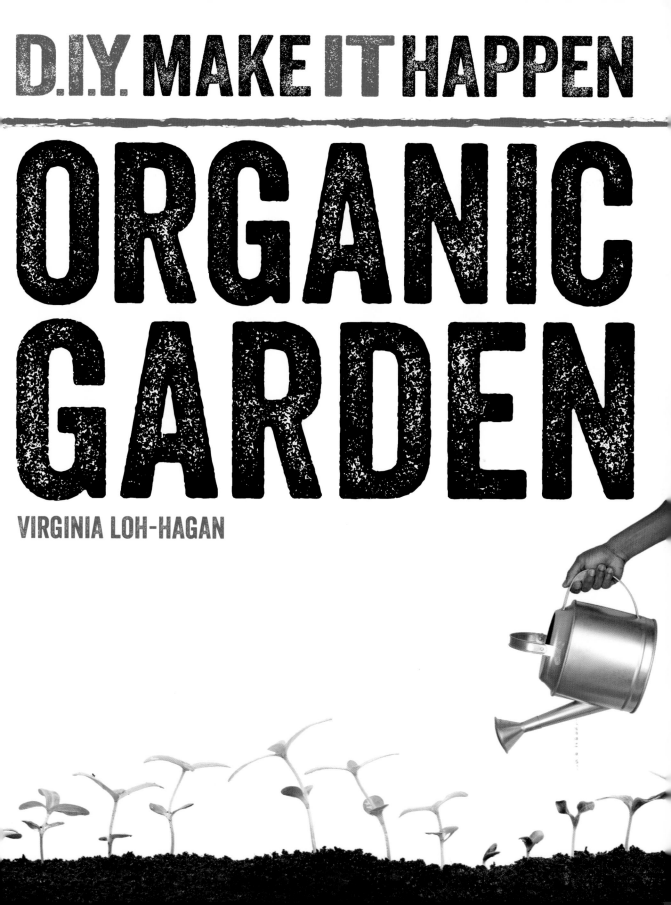

D.I.Y. MAKE IT HAPPEN

ORGANIC GARDEN

VIRGINIA LOH-HAGAN

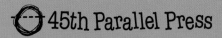
45th Parallel Press

McLEAN MERCER REGIONAL LIBRARY
BOX 505
RIVERDALE, ND 58565

Published in the United States of America by Cherry Lake Publishing
Ann Arbor, Michigan
www.cherrylakepublishing.com

Reading Adviser: Marla Conn MS, Ed., Literacy specialist, Read-Ability, Inc.
Book Designer: Felicia Macheske

Photo Credits: Photo Credits: © Paladin12/Shutterstock.com, cover, 1, 12; © photka/Shutterstock.com, cover, 1, 20; © vesna cvorovic/Shutterstock.com, 3; © stockphoto mania/Shutterstock.com, 5; © Aleksandr Kurganov/Shutterstock.com, 7; © jps/Shutterstock.com, 7, 31; © Simone van den Berg/Shutterstock.com, 9; © ARENA Creative/Shutterstock.com, 10; © Nils Z/Shutterstock.com, 12; © ajlatan/Shutterstock.com, 15; © Macromanaic/Shutterstock.com, 16, 30; © Eric Isselee/Shutterstock.com, 17; © Pixavril/Shutterstock.com, 18; © Pan Xunbin/Shutterstock.com, 19; © kzww/Shutterstock.com, 19; © Monkey Business Images/Shutterstock.com, 21; © Bonnie Taylor Barry/Shutterstock.com, 23; © Scisetti Alfio/Shutterstock.com, 24, 31; © Viacheslav Nikolaenko/Shutterstock.com, 26; © raulbaenacasado/Shutterstock.com, 27; © Jorgegrafias/Shutterstock.com, 28; © Josep Curto/Shutterstock.com, 29; © wavebreakmedia/Shutterstock.com, back cover; © Dora Zett/Shutterstock.com, back cover

Graphic Elements: © IreneArt/Shutterstock.com, 4, 8; © pashabo/Shutterstock.com, 6; © axako/Shutterstock.com, 7; © Katya Bogina/Shutterstock.com, 11, 17; © Fandorina Liza/Shutterstock.com, 11, 20, 25; © Belausava Volha/Shutterstock.com, 12, 18; © Nik Merkulov/Shutterstock.com, 13; © Ya Tshey/Shutterstock.com, 14, 25; © kubais/Shutterstock.com, 16; © Ursa Major/Shutterstock.com, 21, 26; © Sasha Nazim/Shutterstock.com, 22, 29; © Infomages/Shutterstock.com, 24; © Art'nLera/Shutterstock.com, back cover

Copyright © 2017 by Cherry Lake Publishing
All rights reserved. No part of this book may be reproduced or utilized in any
form or by any means without written permission from the publisher.

45th Parallel Press is an imprint of Cherry Lake Publishing.

Library of Congress Cataloging-in-Publication Data

Names: Loh-Hagan, Virginia, author. I Loh-Hagan, Virginia. D.I.Y. Make it happen.
Title: Organic garden / by Virginia Loh-Hagan.
Description: Ann Arbor : Cherry Lake Publishing, [2016] I Series: D.I.Y. Make
   it happen I Includes bibliographical references and index.
Identifiers: LCCN 2016001529I ISBN 9781634711029 (hardcover) I ISBN
   9781634712019 (pdf) I ISBN 9781634713009 (pbk.) I ISBN 9781634713993 (ebook)
Subjects: LCSH: Organic gardening—Juvenile literature.
Classification: LCC SB453.5 .L64 2016 I DDC 635.9/87—dc23
LC record available at http://lccn.loc.gov/2016001529

Cherry Lake Publishing would like to acknowledge the work of The Partnership for 21st Century Skills.
Please visit *www.p21.org* for more information.

Printed in the United States of America
Corporate Graphics Inc.

ABOUT THE AUTHOR

Dr. Virginia Loh-Hagan is an author, university professor, former classroom teacher, and curriculum designer. She would love to grow her own gardens but does not have a green thumb. She's killed every plant she's owned. She lives in San Diego with her very tall husband and very naughty dogs. To learn more about her, visit www.virginialoh.com.

TABLE OF CONTENTS

CHAPTER ONE

WHAT DOES IT MEAN TO GROW AN ORGANIC GARDEN?

Do you love plants? Do you love watching things grow? Do you have a green thumb? Then creating an **organic** garden is the right project for you!

Having a green thumb means having **gardening** skills. Gardening is growing plants. **Gardeners** garden. They dig dirt. They plant seeds. They water. They **weed**. Weeding is pulling out unwanted plants. They **harvest**. Harvest means gathering crops.

Organic means natural. Organic gardeners only use natural things. They keep the soil healthy. They keep plants healthy. They don't add chemicals to soil. They don't use chemical **fertilizers**. Fertilizers are added to soil. They help plants grow.

Talk to other organic gardeners. Get their opinions.

KNOW THE LINGO

Annuals: plants that grow and die in the same season

Bedding out: planting plants in beds

Biennials: plants that complete their life cycle in two growing seasons

Biodegradable: materials that break down into smaller bits through a natural process

Bolt: when vegetables stop making new leaves and send up stalks, turning the remaining leaves bitter

Cultivate: digging in the dirt and preparing the land for planting

Deadheading: removing dead or faded flowers

Foliage: a plant's leaves

Full sun: gardens that get sun for 7 to 8 hours

Part sun: gardens that get some sun and some shade throughout the day

Perennials: plants that continue growing from season to season

Rootbound: when the roots of potted plants wrap around the bottom of the pot

Sport: a plant part that is different from the rest of the plant

Volunteers: plants that grow where they're not planted

Organic gardeners don't use **pesticides**. Pesticides are chemicals used to kill bugs. Pesticides are linked to health problems.

Organic gardeners grow healthy foods. They grow healthy flowers. They use **sustainable** practices. This means they use natural resources. They help the environment. They help wildlife. They work with nature.

You'll have fun creating your own organic garden. You'll play in the dirt. You'll watch your plants grow. The best part is you can eat the food you grow!

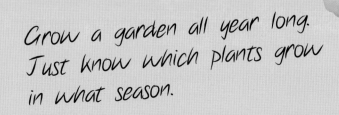

Grow a garden all year long. Just know which plants grow in what season.

CHAPTER TWO

WHAT DO YOU NEED TO GROW AN ORGANIC GARDEN?

Get tools. Gardeners need gear to garden.

- ⇒ **A trowel.** It has a flat, pointed blade. It scoops dirt. It lifts plants.

- ⇒ **Weeding tools.** They help gardeners pull out weeds.

- ⇒ **A hoe.** It has a long handle. It has a thin metal blade. It weeds. It breaks up soil.

- ⇒ **Pruners.** They're like scissors. They clip plants.

- ⇒ **A fork.** It's like a rake. It prepares the soil.

- ⇒ **A spade.** It's a hand shovel. It's used to dig.

Protect your skin. Gardeners work outside a lot.

➡ **Wear a hat.**

➡ **Wear sunscreen.**

➡ **Wear sunglasses.**

➡ **Wear gardening gloves.**

➡ **Cover your arms and legs.**

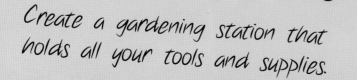

Create a gardening station that holds all your tools and supplies.

Decide the garden size.

➡ **Think small at first. Small gardens are easier.**

➡ **Consider a garden that's 4 feet by 4 feet (1.2 meters by 1.2 m). It provides enough food for one person.**

➡ **Consider using pots. Or use small containers.**

Choose a **bed** for your garden. Beds are areas used for planting. There are different options for garden sites.

➡ Plant outside. Find a place that gets sun. Herbs and vegetables need over **6 hours** of sun each day. Find a place with good **drainage**. Drainage means getting rid of extra water. Pull out any weeds.

➡ Plant inside. Grow plants in a small box. Place it by the window.

Study the site. See how much sun it gets.

Get seeds, **seedlings**, or plants. Seedlings are young plants. Organic gardeners choose the right plants for the right place. They grow **native** plants. They grow plants that naturally grow in the area. These plants have few **pest** problems. Pests are bugs.

➡ Think about your area. Is it rainy? Is it dry? Certain plants grow better in certain areas.

➡ Consider growing herbs. Herbs grow in any soil. They're used in cooking. They flavor food.

➡ Consider growing tomatoes, lettuce, beans, onions, and strawberries. They're the easiest vegetables and fruits to grow.

➡ Consider growing root plants. These include carrots, beets, and radishes. Consider growing potatoes. They're **tubers**. Roots and tubers grow best in cool weather.

Learn about plants. There are many different types.

TRY THIS!

Create eggheads with plant hair!

You'll need: one egg, art supplies, half of a toilet paper roll, soil, grass seeds

Steps

1 Make a big hole in the egg top. Get rid of the insides. Clean out the shell.

2 Draw a face. (Add funny eyes.)

3 Put eggshell on toilet paper roll. Make sure hole is on top.

4 Fill eggshell with soil.

5 Sprinkle in grass seeds. (Or grow herbs. Or grow cat grass for hungry cats.)

6 Provide water and sunlight.

7 Watch the egghead grow plant hair! (It'll grow in 4 to 5 days. Trim to keep it growing for weeks.)

8 Transplant to garden or bigger pot. Break away the eggshell.

CHAPTER THREE

HOW DO YOU SET UP AN ORGANIC GARDEN?

Use good soil. Soil is important. It feeds plants. It protects plants. Healthy soil makes healthy plants. Healthy plants fight pests. They fight sickness.

Test the soil. Take a handful of soil. Squeeze it. Open your hand. Three things can happen.

➡ **The soil holds its shape. Poke it. It crumbles. This is good soil.**

➡ **The soil holds its shape. Poke it. It doesn't move. This is clay-based soil. It's not good for gardening.**

➡ **The soil falls apart. It's sandy. It's bad soil.**

But that's okay. Organic gardeners can make good soil out of bad soil. They feed the soil. They make it better.

Feed the soil. The soil feeds the plants!

Advice from the Field
MICHAEL W. TWITTY

Michael W. Twitty is a food writer and historian. He studies African American food traditions. African Americans have organic farming in their history. He said, "No one had to tell me about organic or sustainable because that was the tradition that was passed down to me." African American families gardened because they had to feed their families. Kitchen gardens were important to their daily lives. These gardens weren't a hobby. They were for survival. He wants more African Americans to garden. He said, "Improve [land] through organic means and grow our heirlooms and raise our heritage breeds." He wants people to grow foods that are part of their cultures. He said, "This is a call to action. ... So the first action is to grow what you can."

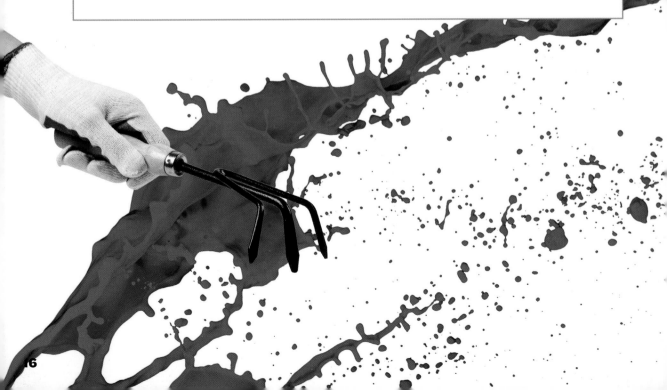

Make a **compost** pile. Compost makes good soil. It makes soil healthier. It makes soil better able to hold water. It's made from natural things.

→ Collect "green" things. These things are wet. They're high in nitrogen. Get vegetable and fruit scraps. Get coffee grinds. Get tea leaves. Get grass clippings. Get plants.

→ Collect "brown" things. These things are dry. They're high in carbon. Get leaves. Get straw and hay. Get wood chips. Get paper. Get egg and nut shells. Get hair. Get paper towels and tubes.

→ Put these things together. Put them in a bin.

→ Wait. Let these things break down. Let them rot.

→ Mix the pile.

→ Put compost on top of garden beds.

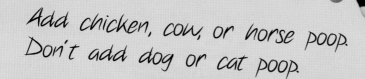

Add chicken, cow, or horse poop. Don't add dog or cat poop.

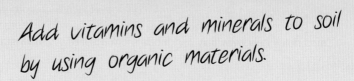

Add vitamins and minerals to soil by using organic materials.

Always keep the soil healthy.

⮕ Let the land become **fallow**. Fallow means giving soil a rest. Vegetables and flowers can't grow all the time. This usually happens in fall and winter.

⮕ Rotate crops. Plant different plants each year. This keeps pests away. This keeps the soil healthy.

⮕ Encourage earthworms. Cover soil with compost. Earthworms will come. They like good soil. They eat rotting things. They increase air space in soil. They poop. They pee. Earthworm poop and pee is called "worm tea." It's good for gardens.

Build the garden. Plant your plants.

➡ **Think about spacing. Keep plants close together. This stops weed growth. It helps soil keep water. But don't put them too close. This will make it easier to spread sickness.**

➡ **Decide to plant in rows or in groups.**

➡ **Dig holes. Dig as deep as the width of the seed or plant.**

➡ **Sow the seeds in the holes. Sow means scatter. Or place plants or seedlings in the holes.**

➡ **Fill the hole. Cover with soil.**

➡ **Pat the area down.**

➡ **Water it a lot.**

➡ **Cover the soil with compost. Or use mulch. Mulch is rotting leaves or bark.**

Make beds 3 weeks
before planting.

CHAPTER FOUR

HOW DO YOU MAINTAIN AN ORGANIC GARDEN?

Use natural ways to get rid of pests. Pests hurt plants. They can kill plants. Organic farmers don't use bug spray. Bug spray has poisons.

➡ Encourage good bugs. These include ladybird beetles and praying mantis. Learn about bugs. There are good bugs. There are bad bugs. Bad bugs include ants and aphids. Good bugs help control bad bugs. They eat bug eggs.

➡ Handpick bad bugs away. Turn over leaves. Check for bugs. Check for eggs.

- ➡ **Plant carrots in toilet paper rolls. This keeps away bad worms.**

- ➡ **Plant peppermint and spearmint. Bad bugs hate mint.**

- ➡ **Cook cedar twigs in water. Let the water cool. Pour it over plants. It keeps bugs away.**

Encourage birds and toads. They eat bugs.

QUICK TIPS

- Put tinfoil around the base of plants. This keeps out bad bugs.

- Don't compost sick or infested plants.

- Get plants with thick leaves. These plants don't need a lot of water.

- Make compost tea. Mix compost and water. Then, let it sit. Pour this onto the soil around plants.

- Collect plastic containers. Place them over plants. Use them as covers. This protects plants from frost.

- Test soil before watering. Push your index finger two knuckles deep into the soil. If it feels damp, don't water.

- Water seedlings a lot. They have small root systems. They need more water. Trees, shrubs, and perennials find water with their deep roots.

Talk to plants. Some believe plants grow better when talked to.

Water plants. Organic gardeners protect water as well. Water is a natural resource.

⇒ **Water deeply and completely. But watering too much is not good. Watering just the top is not good. Train plants to build deep roots. This will help them live longer.**

⇒ **Capture and store rainwater.**

⇒ **Water early morning. Or water early evening. This saves water. Don't let the sun dry up the water.**

⇒ **Use mulch. This holds water.**

Check gardens regularly.

⇒ **Use your thumb and forefinger. Pinch off side shoots. These are sprouts. Pinching keeps the plant full.**

⇒ **Cut back some plants. Don't let plants grow too tall. Don't let plants flop. Cut stems.**

Control weeds. Weeds can take over gardens. They stop plants from growing.

➡ **Use a hoe. Cut off the green parts.**

➡ **Pull weeds by hand. Remove the roots.**

➡ **Use heat. This helps control weeds that grow in cracks. Pour boiling water on the weeds.**

Collect seeds. Save them. Use the seeds in next year's garden.

➡ **Leave flower heads on plants. Let seeds fully grow.**

➡ **Cut the toe from panty hose. Put this over the flower. Tie it on. This catches the seeds. For fruits, cut them open. Pull out the seeds. Wash them.**

➡ **Dry seeds. Spread seeds on a plate.**

➡ **Keep in an envelope. Label them.**

Use your own natural resources.

Harvest the gardens. Finally, plants produced food!

➡ **Collect produce. Produce means fruits and vegetables. Pull the food off plants.**

➡ **Use a laundry basket. It's like a strainer. Water the basket. Rinse off dirt. Dirty water strains out.**

What to do with all your produce?

➡ **Eat it raw. Cook it. Enjoy all your hard work.**

➡ **Trade your produce. Other organic farmers may grow different things. Trade your produce for theirs.**

➡ **Sell your produce. Consider getting a booth at the farmers' market. A booth is a station or area.**

➡ **Give it away! Give it as gifts to friends and family. Help feed the homeless.**

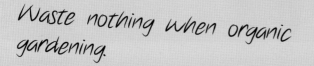

Waste nothing when organic gardening.

D.I.Y. EXAMPLE!

STEPS	EXAMPLES
When	◆ Start growing organic garden in late spring. ◆ Start composting 3 weeks before planting.
Where	◆ Use the sunniest spot in the backyard. ◆ Use the spot close to the water hose. ◆ Place the compost bin close to this area.
How	◆ Create raised beds. Raised beds are garden boxes. They're made with wood. They have four sides. They're great for small gardens. They keep away weeds. They provide good drainage. They serve as a barrier to pests like slugs and snails. ◆ Group plants in a grid. Label each group.

STEPS	EXAMPLES
Size	◆ Create a bed that's about 2 feet (0.6 m) long and 2 feet (0.6 m) wide.
Why	◆ To grow all the ingredients needed to make guacamole, except for avocados. (The neighbor grows avocados. I'll trade my produce for some avocados.)
Plants	◆ Cilantro ◆ Tomatoes ◆ Yellow onions ◆ Spring onions ◆ Serrano peppers ◆ Garlic

GLOSSARY

bed (BED) area used for planting

booth (BOOTH) a sale station or area

compost (KAHM-pohst) natural fertilizer

drainage (DRAY-nij) getting rid of extra water

fallow (FAL-oh) letting soil rest by not using it to plant

fertilizers (FUR-tuh-lye-zurz) natural or artificial substances added to soil to make it grow plants

fork (FORK) tool that looks like a rake used to prepare the soil

gardeners (GAHR-duhn-urz) people who garden

gardening (GAHR-duhn-ing) growing plants

harvest (HAHR-vist) to gather crops or produce

hoe (HOH) tool with a long handle and thin metal blade used to break up soil and to weed

mulch (MULCH) rotting leaves or bark used as fertilizer

native (NAY-tiv) plants that grow naturally in an area

organic (or-GAN-ik) natural

pest (PEST) bad bug that hurts plants

pesticides (PES-tih-sydz) chemicals used to kill pests or bugs

produce (PROH-doos) fruits and vegetables

pruners (PROON-urz) tools that look like scissors used to clip plants

seedlings (SEED-lingz) young plants

sow (SOH) sprinkle or scatter

spade (SPAYD) hand shovel used to dig

sustainable (suh-STAY-nuh-buhl) using natural resources and not destroying anything in nature

trowel (TROU-uhl) tool with a flat, pointed blade used to scoop dirt or lift plants

tubers (TOO-burz) plants like potatoes

weed (WEED) to pull out unwanted plants

INDEX

LEARN MORE

BOOKS

Scholl, Elizabeth. *Organic Gardening for Kids*. Hockessin, DE: Mitchell Lane Publishing, 2009.

Whitman, Ann, Suzanne DeJohn, and the Editors of the National Gardening Association. *Organic Gardening for Dummies*. Hoboken, NJ: Wiley Publishing, 2009.

WEB SITES

National Gardening Association: www.garden.org

National Wildlife Federation—Garden for Wildlife: Organic Gardening: www.nwf.org/How-to-Help/Garden-for-Wildlife/Gardening-Tips/Organic-Gardening.aspx